Nuñez

Skill-Building
Morning
Jumpstarts

by Deborah Poston and Grainger Shearin

SCHOLASTIC
PROFESSIONAL BOOKS

New York • Toronto • London • Auckland • Sydney Mexico City • New Delhi • Hong Kong

We would like to dedicate this book to the students in our classes at Fairfield Primary School in Winnsboro, South Carolina (1992–2000).

Cover design by Sue Kass and Norma Ortiz

Interior design by Ellen Hassell for Boultinghouse & Boultinghouse, Inc.

Cover and interior illustrations by Mike Moran

ISBN: 0-439-13116-2

Contents

Introduction

Welcome to *Skill-Building Morning Jumpstarts*! These 50 fun, reproducible activity sheets are a great way to get kids focused, on task, and ready for learning—in the morning, after lunch, at the end of the school day, or during any other transition time. Each double-sided sheet reinforces essential skills with quick exercises, such as Sentence Busters, Magic Numbers, Analogy of the Day, and more. The consistent format of the activity sheets helps kids work independently and with confidence. While kids are working on their own, you can take attendance, answer questions, pass out papers, or otherwise effect a smooth transition into the next activity.

Jumpstarts are a great way to prepare kids for standardized tests. Each activity sheet builds skills in key areas: math, vocabulary, writing, punctuation, problem solving, and more. Although the format remains consistent, the sheets gradually increase in complexity and build on skills covered in previous sheets. Each sheet includes the following skill-building sections:

- **Magic Number**—Reviews place value and number sense

- **Math Busters**—Builds essential skills such as addition, subtraction, time, money, patterns, simple fractions, and more

- **Sentence Busters**—Reviews capitalization, punctuation, mechanics, spelling, and more

- **Analogy of the Day**—Builds comparative skills as kids analyze relationships between words

- **Word of the Day**—Expands vocabularies with useful new words

- **Think Tank**—Word problems that develop problem solving, math, and language arts skills

- **Splash into Handwriting**—Gives kids practice using their best print or cursive

- **Brainteaser**—Fun problems and puzzles that exercise creativity

Jumpstarts are designed to be a versatile learning tool for second through fourth graders. Please refer to the section below entitled "How to Use This Book" for suggestions on how to help students get the most out of these activity sheets. In the back of the book on pages 107–112, you'll find an answer key.

We hope that you enjoy Jumpstarts as much as we have enjoyed developing them!

How to Use This Book

Skill-Building Morning Jumpstarts can be used in a variety of ways. In this section, we'll share how we used them most effectively in our classroom. We encourage you to adapt the program to meet the needs and learning styles of your students.

Jumpstarts are a wonderful way to get kids focused at the beginning of the school day. Using these activity sheets as a morning routine helps children feel a sense of purpose as soon as they enter the classroom. Or you can use Jumpstarts at other times when you would like to get kids back on task, such as after lunch or at the end of the school day. It is most effective to have all your students work on Jumpstarts at the same time. Since Jumpstarts are intended for independent use, it is important to look them over in advance to make sure that you have covered the skills needed to complete them. You can have children skip sections, if necessary, and then complete those sections later as part of a whole-group lesson.

Since children will complete their activity sheets at different rates, it is important to specify what they should do when they are finished. A suggested activity is quiet reading, so that other students can continue their work without interruption. When everyone has finished, review the answers on the Jumpstart as a group. Reviewing answers right away provides extra reinforcement of the skills and allows children to ask questions while they are fresh in their minds. We suggest having children correct their own papers, using a different color pencil.

We give our students a Jumpstart activity sheet each day, Monday through Thursday. On Thursday, we ask our students to staple together the four sheets from the week. Then we review information from these Jumpstarts that will be included on a quiz on Friday or Monday. Students highlight the information they need to study, so that the Jumpstarts become handy study sheets. This simple routine encourages good study habits (plus, using highlighters makes kids feel very mature!).

When you first introduce Jumpstarts, walk students through each section so that they understand the directions. Give each student a double-sided copy of the first Jumpstart. If desired, make overhead transparencies of both sides. (You may want to go over Side A one day and Side B the next.) It is a good idea to work through the first few Jumpstarts as a group until children are comfortable with the routine and ready to work independently. Although children will need more time to complete the first few Jumpstarts, once a routine is established

most children will be able to complete a Jumpstart in 10 to 20 minutes. Following are section-by-section suggestions for using Jumpstarts.

Magic Number
This section reinforces place value and number sense. A number is written in a grid that shows the place value of each digit. The magic number is the bold-faced digit. First, children write the place value of the magic number. Then, show children how to write the entire number in expanded form. For example, they would write 577 as 500 + 70 + 7. Next, children write the number in words (*five hundred seventy-seven*).

Math Busters
In this section, children practice essential skills to solve math problems (addition, subtraction, patterns, time, money, multiplication, simple fractions, and more). It is a good idea to review Math Busters in advance to make sure that you have covered the skills kids need to complete this section. Math Busters are usually comprised of three short problems or groups of problems.

Sentence Busters
This section includes two incorrect sentences. Students find the errors and rewrite the sentences so that they are correct. They will find errors in capitalization, punctuation, verb tense, and spelling. Encourage students to be on the lookout for any kind of mistakes! You may need to review skills in advance so that students will be familiar with using a particular punctuation mark, capitalization rule, and so on. The answer key provides possible answers, but answers may vary.

Analogy of the Day
Children will feel very grown up if you tell them that even adults face analogies on

tests to enter college and graduate school! The simple analogies provided in Jumpstarts are a friendly and fun way to introduce children to this skill. Explain that an analogy is a comparison. An analogy describes how pairs of words are related.

Show students several simple examples, such as *sun is to day as moon is to ____.* To find the answer, students need to determine the relationship between *sun* and *day*. A good strategy is to think of a sentence that describes the relationship, such as "The sun shines during the day." Then, plug *moon* into the same sentence. (*"The moon shines during the ____."*) The answer, of course, is *night*. When you are reviewing the answers to Jumpstarts, always ask children to share the sentence that describes the relationship between the first pair of words.

Word of the Day

The Word of the Day appears in bold, followed by a simple definition. Please note that some words may have additional meanings. One definition is provided to be as clear as possible. You may want to discuss other meanings or connotations as you see fit. For extra reinforcement, it is helpful to "act out" the word with a body movement or facial expression. You may also want to use this section as a springboard to discuss parts of speech. For example, you can discuss how the verb *explain* can be turned into a noun by changing the word to *explanation*.

Encourage children to use the Word of the Day in a sentence that shows the meaning of the word. This may be challenging for children, but it will prompt them to think about the meaning and write more thoughtful sentences. Explain that using details and parts of the definition in their sentences helps to show the meaning. Sample

sentences are provided in the answer key.

Think Tank

In this section, kids apply problem solving, math, and language arts skills to solve a variety of word problems. The math questions involve addition, subtraction, time, money, fractions, graphing, and more. Language arts questions ask children to use their knowledge of parts of speech, homophones, antonyms, synonyms, and more. Kids will enjoy the diversity of this section, and they'll also see how they can apply their skills in a variety of ways. Encourage kids to answer questions in complete sentences, or at least to be specific in their answers. For example, rather than simply stating an answer as 15, encourage kids to write "15 books" or "She had 15 books." This section is especially helpful for standardized test preparation.

Splash into Handwriting

In this section, children are given five words to write in either their best print or cursive. Wide write-on lines are provided for extra guidance. If you wish, you can have kids start with printing at the beginning of the year and move on to cursive later in the year.

Brainteaser

Brainteasers encourage kids to use their creative side. Similar to Think Tank, there are a variety of types of questions. Kids will unscramble words, draw inventions, write poems, solve word searches, and more. Brainteasers also incorporate a range of math and language arts skills, so that kids continue to hone their skills while they are having fun!

Name _____ Date _____

✨Magic Number✨

The magic number is in the

_____ place.

ten-thousands	thousands	hundreds	tens	ones
		5	7	7

Expanded Form: _____

Words: _____

Math Busters

What time is it?

What time is it?

What time will it be in one hour?

_____   _____   _____

Sentence Busters Rewrite these sentences so that they are correct.

1. today we will learn about numbers?

_____

2. do you have a pet shark

_____

ANALOGY of the Day

Smell is to **nose** as **see** is to _____.

WORD of the Day Use the word in a sentence.

masterpiece: a great piece of work, such as a painting or book

_____

_____

THINK TANK

There are 11 clowns at the carnival. If each clown has 3 buttons, how many buttons do the clowns have in all?

Answer: _____

Splash into Handwriting

time

word

sentence

clown

button

Brainteaser

How many triangles are in this picture?

Answer: _____

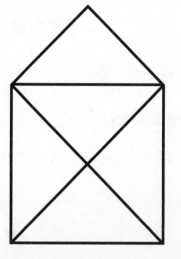

Skill-Building Morning Jumpstarts   Scholastic Professional Books

Name _____ Date _____

✨Magic Number✨

The magic number is in the

_____ place.

ten-thousands	thousands	hundreds	tens	ones
		4	8	6

Expanded Form: _____

Words: _____

Math Busters

Fill in the missing numbers in the patterns.

1, 2, _____, _____, 5

56, _____, 58, _____, 60

25, 24, _____, 22, _____

Sentence Busters Rewrite these sentences so that they are correct.

1. how many days are in a week

_____

2. sally jeff and ashley went to the zoo

_____

ANALOGY of the Day

△ is to ○ as ▲ is to _____.

WORD of the Day Use the word in a sentence.

moist: slightly wet

_____

_____

Side B

THINK TANK

You have 12 muffins and your family eats 4. You give your best friend 3. How many do you have left?

Answer: _____

Splash into Handwriting

week

day

triangle

square

circle

Brainteaser

Draw a picture using only three squares, two triangles, and one circle. What did you make?

I made a _____.

10

Name _____ Date _____

✨ Magic Number ✨

The magic number is in the

_____ place.

ten-thousands	thousands	hundreds	tens	ones
	7,	2	9	0

Expanded Form: _____

Words: _____

Math Busters

5 + 4 = ____   3 + 4 = ____   9 – 3 = ____

6 + 5 = ____   7 + 5 = ____   8 – 5 = ____

Sentence Busters Rewrite these sentences so that they are correct.

1. yes the book is in the library

_____

2. charlotte's web is a great book

_____

ANALOGY of the Day

Drink is to **thirsty** as **eat** is to _____ .

WORD of the Day Use the word in a sentence.

peculiar: odd or strange

_____

_____

THINK TANK

Karen sold fewer tickets than Marie.
Marie sold more tickets than Frank.
Frank sold more tickets than Karen
but fewer tickets than Joshua. Who
sold the fewest tickets?

Answer: _____

Splash into Handwriting

eat

five

ticket

number

peculiar

Brainteaser

Write a large number 5.
Then draw details to turn
it into an animal.

Skill-Building Morning Jumpstarts   Scholastic Professional Books

Name _____ Date _____

✧Magic Number✧

The magic number is in the

_____ place.

ten-thousands	thousands	hundreds	tens	ones
2	4,	6	8	9

Expanded Form: _____

Words: _____

Math Busters

7 – 4 = ___   3 + 6 = ___   8 – 4 = ___

6 – 4 = ___   8 + 9 = ___   9 – 2 = ___

Sentence Busters   Rewrite these sentences so that they are correct.

1. we goes to the movie after school on thursday

_____

2. jerry loves broccoli spinach and carrots

_____

ANALOGY of the Day

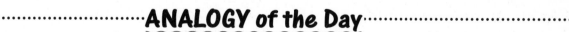

Lemon is to **sour** as **sugar** is to _____.

WORD of the Day   Use the word in a sentence.

combine: to mix or join things together

_____

THINK TANK

List the days of the week in alphabetical order.

_____

_____

_____

_____

_____

Splash into Handwriting

Thursday

Friday

comma

combine

movie

Brainteaser

Unscramble the following letters to form words:

rTsydhau _____   Fydari _____

Skill-Building Morning Jumpstarts   Scholastic Professional Books

Name _____ Date _____

✰Magic Number✰

The magic number is in the

_____ place.

ten-thousands	thousands	hundreds	tens	ones
	1,	**1**	**7**	**5**

Expanded Form: _____

Words: _____

Math Busters

254

☐ odd

☐ even

1,230

☐ odd

☐ even

3,745

☐ odd

☐ even

Sentence Busters Rewrite these sentences so that they are correct.

1. dan can you name the oceans

_____

2. the atlantic ocean is a large body of water

_____

ANALOGY of the Day

A is to **a** as **B** is to _____.

WORD of the Day Use the word in a sentence.

antonym: a word whose meaning is the opposite of another word

_____

THINK TANK

Write five words and their antonyms. For example: **up** and **down**.

_____   _____

_____   _____

_____   _____

_____   _____

Splash into Handwriting

even

odd

ocean

body

water

Brainteaser

Write two words whose letters fit into this shape.

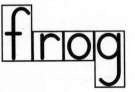 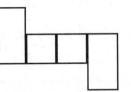 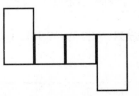

Skill-Building Morning Jumpstarts   Scholastic Professional Books

Name _____ Date _____

✧Magic Number✧

The magic number is in the

_____ place.

ten-thousands	thousands	hundreds	tens	ones
		3	5	7

Expanded Form: _____

Words: _____

Math Busters

5 + 5 = ___   6 + 6 = ___

5 + 5 + 5 = ___   6 + 6 + 6 = ___

5 + 5 + 5 + 5 + 5 = ___   6 + 6 + 6 + 6 = ___

Sentence Busters Rewrite these sentences so that they are correct.

1. the boy was sitting the grass

_____

2. i will give the present to patrick

_____

ANALOGY of the Day

Foot is to **toes** as **hand** is to _____.

WORD of the Day Use the word in a sentence.

pattern: an arrangement of shapes, colors, or lines that repeats

_____

_____

THINK TANK

Ms. Jones went to a yard sale
and bought a stuffed animal
for $1.00, a vase for $2.00,
and two clocks for $1.00 each.
How much did she spend in all?

Answer: _____

Splash into Handwriting

foot

pattern

sale

book

library

Brainteaser

Fill in the blanks to complete the patterns.

     _____ _____

    _____ _____

JUMPSTART 7

Side A

Name _____ Date _____

✦Magic Number✦

The magic number is in the

_____ place.

ten-thousands	thousands	hundreds	tens	ones
		2	8	5

Expanded Form: _____

Words: _____

Math Busters

What time is it?	What time is it?	What time will it be in 30 minutes?

_____	_____	_____

Sentence Busters   Rewrite these sentences so that they are correct.

1. katy will going to the store

_____

2. do you want to go with she

_____

ANALOGY of the Day

◯ is to ● as ▢ is to _____ .

WORD of the Day   Use the word in a sentence.

brief: lasting a short period of time

_____

_____

THINK TANK

Tina is second in a line of seven children. Katy is directly behind her, then John, and then Al. How many children are behind Al? (You can draw a picture to help you figure out the answer.)

Answer: _____

Splash into Handwriting

time

clock

hour

minute

second

Brainteaser

Make this picture symmetrical.

Example:

Skill-Building Morning Jumpstarts   Scholastic Professional Books

Name _____ Date _____

✰Magic Number✰

The magic number is in the

_____ place.

ten-thousands	thousands	hundreds	tens	ones
			1	9

Expanded Form: _____

Words: _____

Math Busters

What number comes before 200?	What number comes after 200?	What number is 100 more than 200?
_____	_____	_____

Sentence Busters Rewrite these sentences so that they are correct.

1. jim went to the store to get apples oranges and banana

_____

2. wen will we get to go outside for recess

_____

ANALOGY of the Day

Sandals are to **summer** as **boots** are to _____.

WORD of the Day   Use the word in a sentence.

sphere: a three-dimensional circular shape, such as a ball

_____

_____

THINK TANK

List as many things as you can that are shaped like spheres.

_____   _____

_____   _____

_____   _____

_____   _____

Splash into Handwriting

sphere

round

ball

circle

picture

Brainteaser

Draw a picture using only circles. (If you want, you can trace something round.)

Skill-Building Morning Jumpstarts   Scholastic Professional Books

Name _____ Date _____

☆Magic Number☆

The magic number is in the

_____ place.

ten-thousands	thousands	hundreds	tens	ones
	6,	5	7	8

Expanded Form: _____

Words: _____

Math Busters

Fill in the missing numbers in the patterns.

2, _____, 6, 8, _____, 12

3, 5, _____, 9, _____, 13

22, _____, 26, 28, _____, 32

Sentence Busters
Rewrite these sentences so that they are correct.

1. we will go to see mrs jefferson today

_____

2. did you read the book green eggs and ham

_____

ANALOGY of the Day

Square is to **cube** as **circle** is to _____.

WORD of the Day
Use the word in a sentence.

grief: a strong feeling of sadness

_____

_____

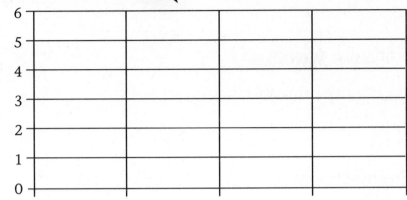

THINK TANK

On the graph, show how kids in Mr. Stanley's class get to school.

6 ride the bus
5 walk
2 skate
4 ride in cars

Splash into Handwriting

graph

data

kids

school

grief

Brainteaser

How many words can you spell using the letters in **communication**? List them here.

main

Name _____ Date _____

☆Magic Number☆

The magic number is in the

_____ place.

ten-thousands	thousands	hundreds	tens	ones
	8,	3	6	7

Expanded Form: _____

Words: _____

Math Busters

Fill in the missing numbers in the patterns.

1, 4, 7, _____, _____, 16

5, 10, _____, _____, 25, 30

101, 102, _____, _____, 105

Sentence Busters

Rewrite these sentences so that they are correct.

1. today I will eat at my aunt judys house

_____

2. tomorrow I will eat at Home

_____

ANALOGY of the Day

Back is to **front** as **left** is to _____.

WORD of the Day

Use the word in a sentence.

fiction: stories that are not true or real

_____

_____

THINK TANK

There are 28 boys in the lunch line.
Bobby is eighth.

How many are in front of him? _____

How many are behind him? _____

Splash into Handwriting

fiction

nonfiction

stories

lunch

sandwich

Brainteaser

Create a sandwich that
you would like to eat.
Draw a picture and then
write what's in it.

26

Name _____ Date _____

✧Magic Number✧

ten-thousands	thousands	hundreds	tens	ones
	2,	1	3	9

The magic number is in the

_____ place.

Expanded Form: _____

Words: _____

Math Busters

Write a number greater than 3 but less than 6.	Write a number greater than 9 but less than 12.	Write a number greater than 100 but less than 110.
_____	_____	_____

Sentence Busters Rewrite these sentences so that they are correct.

1. mr johnson read five newspapers every day

_____

2. have you see my new book

_____

_____

ANALOGY of the Day

☐ is to ☐ as ◐ is to _____.

WORD of the Day Use the word in a sentence.

temporary: lasting only a brief period of time

_____

_____

THINK TANK

Lisa had $2.00 in her piggy bank.
She took out $1.00 and spent $0.50.
How much money does she have left in all?

Answer: _____

Splash into Handwriting

bank

coin

money

cent

dollar

Brainteaser

List as many words as
you can that rhyme
with **hat**. (Hint: Some
rhyming words have
more than three letters.)

_____   _____

_____   _____

_____   _____

_____   _____

_____   _____

Skill-Building Morning Jumpstarts   Scholastic Professional Books

Name _____ Date _____

✧ Magic Number ✧

The magic number is in the

_____ place.

ten-thousands	thousands	hundreds	tens	ones
	3,	4	4	6

Expanded Form: _____

Words: _____

Math Busters

Count the money and write the amount.

_____ | _____ | _____

Sentence Busters

Rewrite these sentences so that they are correct.

1. the dog bark at the cat

_____

2. the cat is jumping on the chair

_____

ANALOGY of the Day

AA BB is to **Aa Bb** as **FF GG** is to _____ .

WORD of the Day

Use the word in a sentence.

synonym: a word whose meaning is the same as another word

_____

THINK TANK

Think of three words and write a synonym for each.
For example: **friend = pal**

_____ = _____

_____ = _____

_____ = _____

Splash into Handwriting

penny

nickel

dime

quarter

buy

Brainteaser

Draw a picture of what you would buy with $12.00. Put price tags on the items and check that they add up to $12.00.

Name _____ Date _____

✨Magic Number✨

The magic number is in the

_____ place.

ten-thousands	thousands	hundreds	tens	ones
	7,	1	5	6

Expanded Form: _____

Words: _____

Math Busters

$$12 + 13$$ $$10 + 30$$ $$11 + 21$$

Sentence Busters Rewrite these sentences so that they are correct.

1. many people like to go to the Movies

_____

2. the Clown knows how to juggles

_____

ANALOGY of the Day

Bird is to **fly** as **fish** is to _____ .

WORD of the Day Use the word in a sentence.

remain: to stay in one place

_____

_____

THINK TANK

Draw lines connecting the shapes with their names.

octagon

square

hexagon

rectangle

Splash into Handwriting

octagon

hexagon

square

rectangle

shape

Brainteaser

Draw a picture using these
shapes: octagons, squares,
hexagons, and rectangles.

JUMPSTART 14

Side A

Name _____ Date _____

✦ Magic Number ✦

The magic number is in the

_____ place.

ten-thousands	thousands	hundreds	tens	ones
		5	4	3

Expanded Form: _____

Words: _____

Math Busters

2,546   7,961   3,450

☐ odd   ☐ odd   ☐ odd

☐ even   ☐ even   ☐ even

Sentence Busters Rewrite these sentences so that they are correct.

1. the Girl is working on a clay pot

_____

2. how many pots has billy maid

_____

ANALOGY of the Day

Apple is to **fruit** as **potato** is to _____.

WORD of the Day Use the word in a sentence.

vast: great size; huge

_____

_____

THINK TANK

Sally found 12 Web sites about sharks. Mark found 4 of the same Web sites and 3 others that Sally did not find. How many different Web sites did they find in all?

Answer: _____

Splash into Handwriting

vast

tiny

clay

pottery

shark

Brainteaser

Fill in the list with things that are vast and things that are tiny.

Vast	Tiny

Skill-Building Morning Jumpstarts   Scholastic Professional Books

Name _____ Date _____

✦Magic Number✦

The magic number is in the

_____ place.

ten-thousands	thousands	hundreds	tens	ones
	3,4	5	9	

Expanded Form: _____

Words: _____

Math Busters

$$26 + 13$$

$$41 + 52$$

$$74 + 25$$

Sentence Busters Rewrite these sentences so that they are correct.

1. did ramon eat any grapes today

_____

2. megan put nine cookie on a tray

_____

ANALOGY of the Day

Sun is to **day** as **moon** is to _____.

WORD of the Day Use the word in a sentence.

examine: to look carefully

_____

_____

THINK TANK

An adjective is a word that describes something or someone.

What adjectives describe you? _____

_____

What adjectives *do not* describe you? _____

_____

Splash into Handwriting

on

off

night

day

opposite

Brainteaser

A verb is a word that tells an action, like **run** or **slip**. List three verbs that you see in this picture.

Skill-Building Morning Jumpstarts Scholastic Professional Books

Name _____ Date _____

✨Magic Number✨

The magic number is in the

_____ place.

ten-thousands	thousands	hundreds	tens	ones
		5	6	7

Expanded Form: _____

Words: _____

Math Busters

$$\begin{array}{r} 57 \\ + 28 \\ \hline \end{array} \qquad \begin{array}{r} 29 \\ + 91 \\ \hline \end{array} \qquad \begin{array}{r} 78 \\ + 33 \\ \hline \end{array}$$

Sentence Busters
Rewrite these sentences so that they are correct.

1. do peter have books

_____

2. yes peter has for books

_____

ANALOGY of the Day

Sheep is to **lamb** as **dog** is to _____.

WORD of the Day
Use the word in a sentence.

unique: one of a kind; special

_____

_____

THINK TANK

Jared is first in the lunch line and Gwen is twelfth. How many people are in between them?

Answer: _____

Splash into Handwriting

do

does

did

was

were

Brainteaser

How many words can you make using the letters in **investigate**? List them here.

state _____

_____ _____

_____ _____

_____ _____

_____ _____

_____ _____

Skill-Building Morning Jumpstarts   Scholastic Professional Books

Name _____ Date _____

✫ Magic Number ✫

The magic number is in the

_____ place.

ten-thousands	thousands	hundreds	tens	ones
	5,	6	7	0

Expanded Form: _____

Words: _____

Math Busters

$$38 - 5$$

$$49 - 11$$

$$52 - 12$$

Sentence Busters — Rewrite these sentences so that they are correct.

1. can the girls run in the race tomorrow

_____

2. the girls can ran in the race on friday

_____

ANALOGY of the Day

→ is to ← as ↑↑ is to _____ .

WORD of the Day   Use the word in a sentence.

vanish: to disappear

_____

_____

THINK TANK

Use these digits to make the greatest number possible, the smallest number possible, and a number with a 2 in the tens place.

2 4 8 7

greatest number: _____

smallest number: _____

2 in tens place: _____

Splash into Handwriting

digit

number

numeral

can

will

Brainteaser

Find and circle these words:

vast

unique

moist

examine

brief

remain

grief

E E G R I E F U
E X R E M A I N
Y B A V M F M I
A W E M O X N Q
E E B R I E F U
Q H C P S N N E
U V A S T T E W

Skill-Building Morning Jumpstarts   Scholastic Professional Books

Name _____ Date _____

✭Magic Number✭

The magic number is in the

_____ place.

ten-thousands	thousands	hundreds	tens	ones
	4,	5	8	7

Expanded Form: _____

Words: _____

Math Busters

Write an even number with two digits.	Write an odd number with three digits.	Write an even number with four digits.
___ ___	___ ___ ___	___ ___ ___ ___

Sentence Busters › Rewrite these sentences so that they are correct.

1. a horse was runing quickly in the meadow

_____

2. did the horse ran quickly in the meadow

_____

ANALOGY of the Day

Month is to **year** as **day** is to _____.

WORD of the Day   Use the word in a sentence.

invent: to create a new thing

_____

THINK TANK

A homophone is a word that sounds the same as another word but has a different spelling and meaning. For example: *to, two,* and *too* are homophones.

How many homophones can you think of? Write them on the lines.

_____

_____

_____

_____

_____

Splash into Handwriting

invent

create

run

ran

running

Brainteaser

What would you like to invent to make your life easier? Draw a picture of your invention and explain to a classmate what it does.

Skill-Building Morning Jumpstarts Scholastic Professional Books

Name _____ Date _____

✨ Magic Number ✨

The magic number is in the

_____ place.

ten-thousands	thousands	hundreds	tens	ones
		6	6	7

Expanded Form: _____

Words: _____

Math Busters

25 − 13	46 − 21	59 − 35

Sentence Busters → Rewrite these sentences so that they are correct.

1. I read a book called arthur's eyes

_____

2. have you read a book that has chapters

_____

ANALOGY of the Day

Girl is to **boy** as **woman** is to _____ .

WORD of the Day   Use the word in a sentence.

voyage: a long trip

_____

_____

THINK TANK

Nine boys and eight girls were invited to a party. Three boys and two girls did not attend. How many children went to the party?

Answer: _____

Splash into Handwriting

boys

girls

children

people

party

Brainteaser

You are having a party for 20 people (including yourself). You would like to make 2 cookies and 1 fruit cup for each person. How many cookies and fruit cups will you need?

Answer: _____

_____

Skill-Building Morning Jumpstarts   Scholastic Professional Books

Name _____ Date _____

✫ Magic Number ✫

The magic number is in the

_____ place.

ten-thousands	thousands	hundreds	tens	ones
4	6,	1	7	0

Expanded Form: _____

Words: _____

Math Busters

Fill in the blanks with <, =, or >.

32 ____ 28   54 ____ 63   1,008 ____ 1,008

Sentence Busters Rewrite these sentences so that they are correct.

1. i like swimming basketball tennis

_____

2. i told you that i would save you a seat

_____

ANALOGY of the Day

Toothbrush is to **teeth** as **hairbrush** is to _____.

WORD of the Day Use the word in a sentence.

carnival: a celebration with games and rides; a fair

_____

_____

THINK TANK

Jackie has 15 books. She lent 2 to
Marty, 3 to Chan, and 1 to her
teacher. How many books does she have left?

Answer: _____

Splash into Handwriting

carnival

games

rides

design

features

Brainteaser

Design a ride for a carnival!
What would your ride look like?
What would it be called? What
special features would it have?
Draw a picture of it at right.

Skill-Building Morning Jumpstarts   Scholastic Professional Books

JUMPSTART 21

Side A

Name _____ Date _____

✦Magic Number✦

The magic number is in the

_____ place.

ten-thousands	thousands	hundreds	tens	ones
2	0,	4	3	5

Expanded Form: _____

Words: _____

Math Busters

Fill in the blanks with <, =, or >.

98 ____ 78   64 ____ 44   23 ____ 54

Sentence Busters Rewrite these sentences so that they are correct.

1. sam has on knew shoes today

_____

2. maya cant wait to go on the field trip

_____

ANALOGY of the Day

Leopard is to **spots** as **zebra** is to _____ .

WORD of the Day Use the word in a sentence.

amaze: to surprise

_____

_____

Skill-Building Morning Jumpstarts Scholastic Professional Books

JUMPSTART 21

Side B

THINK TANK

Compare the amounts of money. Write <, =, or > in the boxes.

Splash into Handwriting

amaze

surprise

leopard

zebra

animal

Brainteaser

If you could design new patterns for a leopard and a zebra, what would they look like? Draw the patterns on the animals.

48

Skill-Building Morning Jumpstarts Scholastic Professional Books

Name _____   Date _____

✦Magic Number✦

The magic number is in the

_____ place.

ten-thousands	thousands	hundreds	tens	ones
	1,	3	5	0

Expanded Form: _____

Words: _____

Math Busters

$$85 - 62$$

$$74 - 65$$

$$97 - 35$$

Sentence Busters Rewrite these sentences so that they are correct.

1. what is the name of your school

_____

2. we dont want to play outside

_____

ANALOGY of the Day

Snake is to **slither** as **frog** is to _____.

WORD of the Day Use the word in a sentence.

triangle: a shape with three angles and three sides

_____

_____

THINK TANK

There are four clowns on the ladder. Gadget is at the top and Ralph is on the very bottom. Chuckles is below Gadget and above Toto.

Can you write the clowns' names in order beside them?

Splash into Handwriting

order

first

second

third

fourth

Brainteaser

Can you spell five words that begin with *A* and have at least five letters? List them here.

Skill-Building Morning Jumpstarts Scholastic Professional Books

Side A

Name _____ Date _____

✦Magic Number✦

The magic number is in the

_____ place.

ten-thousands	thousands	hundreds	tens	ones
1	2,4	4	**8**	7

Expanded Form: _____

Words: _____

Math Busters

$$37 + 67$$

$$92 - 58$$

$$84 + 21$$

Sentence Busters Rewrite these sentences so that they are correct.

1. "why is the sky blue!" asked eddie.

_____

2. where are you going asked Terry.

_____

ANALOGY of the Day

Cow is to **calf** as **cat** is to _____ .

WORD of the Day Use the word in a sentence.

ancient: extremely old

_____

_____

ten-thousands	thousands	hundreds	tens	ones
1	2	4	8	7

THINK TANK

Ronald had a bag of 84 peanuts. A squirrel ate 67 of them. Ronald ate 12 peanuts. How many did he have left?

Answer: _____

Splash into Handwriting

ancient

peanuts

diagram

section

friend

Brainteaser

Compare yourself to a friend or family member. Fill in the Venn diagram with facts about you and your friend or family member. In the middle section, write the things you have in common.

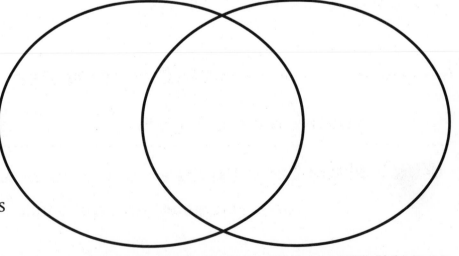

Me

_____
Name of friend or family member

Skill-Building Morning Jumpstarts   Scholastic Professional Books

Name _____ Date _____

☆✦Magic Number✦☆

The magic number is in the

_____ place.

ten-thousands	thousands	hundreds	tens	ones
	8,	4	4	3

Expanded Form: _____

Words: _____

⟨Math Busters⟩   Count the money and write the amount.

_____   _____   _____

⟨Sentence Busters⟩ Rewrite these sentences so that they are correct.

1. when will he bake the cake I asked

_____

2. luis will bake a cake on wenesday

_____

⋯⋯ANALOGY of the Day⋯⋯

Loud is to **quiet** as **high** is to _____.

WORD of the Day   Use the word in a sentence.

variety: a group of several different things

_____

_____

THINK TANK

Grandma sent me $15.00. If I buy a book for $4.00 and a game for $3.50, how much will I have left?

Answer: _____

Splash into Handwriting

birthday

cake

candle

wish

age

Brainteaser

How many words can you make using the letters in **information**? List them here.

roam

_____   _____

_____   _____

_____   _____

_____   _____

_____   _____

Name _____ Date _____

✩Magic Number✩

The magic number is in the

_____ place.

ten-thousands	thousands	hundreds	tens	ones
3	3,	3	3	1

Expanded Form: _____

Words: _____

Math Busters

$$178 + 36$$

$$287 + 158$$

$$708 + 249$$

Sentence Busters Rewrite these sentences so that they are correct.

1. today is thursday said miss johnson

_____

2. it will take to minutes too walk to the park

_____

ANALOGY of the Day

Bird is to **nest** as **spider** is to _____.

WORD of the Day Use the word in a sentence.

uncommon: unique; rare

_____

_____

THINK TANK

Fill in the blanks to complete the patterns.

Splash into Handwriting

for

four

to

two

too

Brainteaser

How many words can
you think of that rhyme
with **ship**? Write them
here.

Skill-Building Morning Jumpstarts Scholastic Professional Books

Name _____ Date _____

✦ Magic Number ✦

The magic number is in the

_____ place.

ten-thousands	thousands	hundreds	tens	ones
	6,	1	4	7

Expanded Form: _____

Words: _____

Math Busters

Laura started work at 8:00 A.M. She worked for five hours. When did she finish? Draw the clock hands.

Start

Finish

Sentence Busters Rewrite these sentences so that they are correct.

1. the boys are named john james joe and jack

_____

2. did you eat a the restaurant today

_____

ANALOGY of the Day

Asleep is to **night** as **awake** is to _____.

WORD of the Day   Use the word in a sentence.

numeral: a symbol for a number, such as *5*

_____

THINK TANK

I have $18.00. The books cost $3.00 each. How many books can I buy?

Answer: _____

Splash into Handwriting

noun

person

place

thing

chart

Brainteaser

A noun names a person, place, or thing. List 15 nouns you can find in your classroom. Write them under the correct heading on the chart.

People	Places	Things
children	art center	chairs

58

Name _____ Date _____

✨Magic Number✨

The magic number is in the

_____ place.

ten-thousands	thousands	hundreds	tens	ones
			9	7

Expanded Form: _____

Words: _____

Math Busters

```
   33          45          24
   22          23          56
 + 11        + 61        + 87
 ____        ____        ____
```

Sentence Busters Rewrite these sentences so that they are correct.

1. you're a terrific friend rebecca

_____

2. did you check you're work

_____

ANALOGY of the Day

Hear is to **ears** as **smell** is to _____.

WORD of the Day Use the word in a sentence.

timid: shy; easily scared

_____

_____

THINK TANK

Draw a line to match each shape with its name.

cube

cylinder

cone

pyramid

Splash into Handwriting

cube

cylinder

cone

pyramid

solid

Brainteaser

Draw a picture that contains a
cube, a cone, and a cylinder.

Skill-Building Morning Jumpstarts Scholastic Professional Books

Name _____ Date _____

✧ Magic Number ✧

The magic number is in the

_____ place.

ten-thousands	thousands	hundreds	tens	ones
	2,	5	9	**2**

Expanded Form: _____

Words: _____

Math Busters

$$313$$
$$-\ \ 21$$

$$438$$
$$-\ 218$$

$$879$$
$$-\ 455$$

Sentence Busters Rewrite these sentences so that they are correct.

1. there are five cats and five dogs in there yard

_____

2. their ant sarah is coming over for dinner

_____

ANALOGY of the Day

Smell is to **odor** as **hear** is to _____.

WORD of the Day Use the word in a sentence.

island: land surrounded on all sides by water

_____

_____

THINK TANK

Beth is taller than Sue. Sue is
taller than Frank. Frank is not
taller than Jack. Jack is taller than
Beth and Sue. Who is the shortest?

Answer: _____

Splash into Handwriting

see

smell

touch

taste

hear

Brainteaser

Fill in the blanks to finish the poem. (It does not have to rhyme.)

I am a(n) _____.
              (KIND OF ANIMAL)

I am _____, _____, and _____.
         (ADJECTIVE)   (ADJECTIVE)   (ADJECTIVE)

I like to _____, _____, and _____,
              (VERB)   (VERB)   (VERB)

and I can _____!
              (VERB)

62

Name _____ Date _____

✦ Magic Number ✦

The magic number is in the

_____ place.

ten-thousands	thousands	hundreds	tens	ones
		1	9	0

Expanded Form: _____

Words: _____

Math Busters

Amanda has 40 cents and Jeremy has 45 cents. How much do they have together?

_____

Jessica has 1 quarter and Pedro has 2 quarters. How many cents do they have together?

_____

Sentence Busters

Rewrite these sentences so that they are correct.

1. Rita ordered a grilled cheese sandwitch.

_____

2. She also ordered desert

_____

ANALOGY of the Day

Snake is to **scales** as **bird** is to _____.

WORD of the Day

Use the word in a sentence.

cause: the reason that something happens

_____

_____

THINK TANK

Sally, Juan, and Maggie are sharing a pizza. They would each like two equal pieces. Draw lines to show how they should cut the pizza.

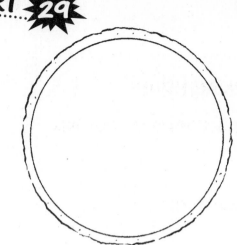

Splash into Handwriting

third

half

fraction

piece

pizza

Brainteaser

Sally likes mushrooms, onions, pepperoni, and extra cheese. Juan likes pepperoni, onions, peppers, mushrooms, and extra cheese. Maggie likes everything except mushrooms and extra cheese. Which pizza toppings would all three of them enjoy?

Answer: _____

_____

64

Name _____ Date _____

✨ Magic Number ✨

The magic number is in the

_____ place.

ten-thousands	thousands	hundreds	tens	ones
		1	**4**	**2**

Expanded Form: _____

Words: _____

Math Busters

$$384 + 256$$

$$667 - 446$$

$$851 - 197$$

Sentence Busters — Rewrite these sentences so that they are correct.

1. ms. Smith fell on mr. Johnson's foot

_____

2. mr Johnsons toe hurt alot

_____

ANALOGY of the Day

Cat is to **meow** as **dog** is to _____.

WORD of the Day — Use the word in a sentence.

rush: to act or move quickly

_____

_____

THINK TANK

How many days were snowy? _____

How many days were rainy? _____

How many more snowy days
were there than rainy days? _____

FEBRUARY

Sunday	Monday	Tuesday	Wednesday	Thursday	Friday	Saturday
	1	2	3	4	5	6
7	8	9	10	11	12	13

Splash into Handwriting

snowy

rainy

sunny

weekend

weather

Brainteaser

Can you list four things that are loud and four things that are quiet?

Loud	**Quiet**
_____	_____
_____	_____
_____	_____
_____	_____

Skill-Building Morning Jumpstarts   Scholastic Professional Books

Name _____ Date _____

✧Magic Number✧

The magic number is in the

_____ place.

ten-thousands	thousands	hundreds	tens	ones
8	8,	2	4	8

Expanded Form: _____

Words: _____

Math Busters

What time is it?	What time will it be in half an hour?	What time was it an hour ago?

_____	_____	_____

Sentence Busters Rewrite these sentences so that they are correct.

1. are lucy mary and kim friends

_____

2. my friend kendall is in third grade?

_____

ANALOGY of the Day

Mother is to **father** as **grandmother** is to _____.

WORD of the Day   Use the word in a sentence.

analyze: to examine or study something carefully

_____

THINK TANK

Draw lines to cut this pizza into 4 pieces.
Draw pepperoni on 1 piece.

What fraction of the
pizza has pepperoni? _____

What fraction does not? _____

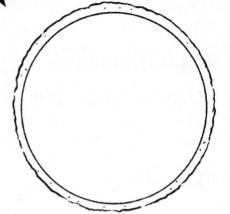

Splash into Handwriting

north

south

west

east

direction

Brainteaser

Jeremy is baking muffins for his class. His recipe
makes 10 muffins, but there are 20 people in his
class (including the teacher). Can you help him
double the ingredients for the recipe and write
how much he will need of each?

___4___ 2 cups flour

_____ 1 cup sugar

_____ 3 tablespoons honey

_____ $\frac{1}{2}$ teaspoon salt

_____ 5 tablespoons butter

_____ $\frac{1}{3}$ cup raisins

68

Name _____ Date _____

✦Magic Number✦

The magic number is in the

_____ place.

ten-thousands	thousands	hundreds	tens	ones
6	0, 7	7	1	

Expanded Form: _____

Words: _____

Math Busters

2 x 2 = ____   4 x 2 = ____   5 x 2 = ____

3 x 3 = ____   4 x 3 = ____   5 x 3 = ____

Sentence Busters ⟩ Rewrite these sentences so that they are correct.

1. Today is my birthday I shouted.

_____

2. my dog max is black and white

_____

ANALOGY of the Day

Fur is to **dogs** as **feathers** are to _____.

WORD of the Day   Use the word in a sentence.

modern: new; up-to-date

_____

_____

THINK TANK

We made 6 cookies. Each cookie had 3 chocolate chips in it. Draw the cookies. How many chocolate chips did we use in all?

Answer: _____

Splash into Handwriting

ones

tens

hundreds

thousands

place value

Brainteaser

Think of ten things you could find at home and at school. Fill in the Venn diagram with the information. In the middle section, write the things you could find in both places.

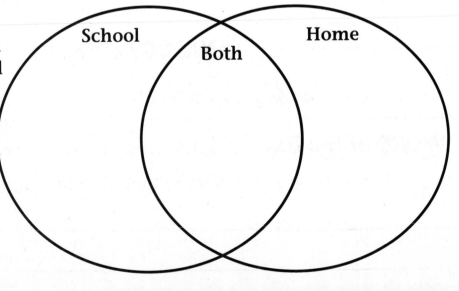

70

Name _____ Date _____

✦Magic Number✦

The magic number is in the

_____ place.

ten-thousands	thousands	hundreds	tens	ones
	1, 8	7	2	

Expanded Form: _____

Words: _____

Math Busters

$ 1.50 + $ 0.50	$ 2.00 + $ 0.75	$ 1.25 + $ 2.25

Sentence Busters Rewrite these sentences so that they are correct.

1. my cat morris and sydney are sweet and playful

_____

2. last year my family went to williamsburg virginia

_____

ANALOGY of the Day

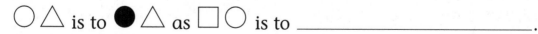 ○△ is to ●△ as □○ is to _____ .

WORD of the Day   Use the word in a sentence.

explain: to give a reason; to make something understandable

_____

_____

THINK TANK

Amy, Leticia, and Tracy want to have their picture taken together. The first copy costs $4.35. Each additional copy costs a dollar. How much will they have to pay in total if they each get a copy of the picture?

Answer: _____

Splash into Handwriting

January

February

March

April

May

Brainteaser

Write the children's birthdays in order on the time line.

Max: June 27, 1995   **Dennis:** April 2, 1995   **Sylvia:** April 23, 1995

Cheryl: January 15, 1995   **Anita:** March 11, 1995

January   February   March   April   May   June

Skill-Building Morning Jumpstarts   Scholastic Professional Books

Name _____ Date _____

☆Magic Number☆

The magic number is in the

_____ place.

ten-thousands	thousands	hundreds	tens	ones
4	4,	9	1	8

Expanded Form: _____

Words: _____

Math Busters

Show 12:30.	Show half past twelve.	Show 30 minutes before 1:00.

Sentence Busters Rewrite these sentences so that they are correct.

1. i hope are teacher feels better tomorrow

_____

2. its a great day to go to the Park

_____

ANALOGY of the Day

▲ is to ▼ as ◄ is to _____ .

WORD of the Day Use the word in a sentence.

collapse: to fall down; to break down

_____

_____

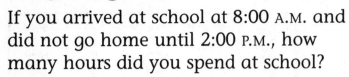

THINK TANK

If you arrived at school at 8:00 A.M. and did not go home until 2:00 P.M., how many hours did you spend at school?

Answer: _____

Splash into Handwriting

August

September

October

November

December

Brainteaser

What is something you can do in an hour?

_____

In half an hour?

_____

In 15 minutes?

_____

In 5 minutes?

_____

Skill-Building Morning Jumpstarts   Scholastic Professional Books

Name _____ Date _____

✦Magic Number✦

The magic number is in the

_____ place.

ten-thousands	thousands	hundreds	tens	ones
7	9, 8	1	7

Expanded Form: _____

Words: _____

Math Busters

$ 1.00 + $ 2.10	$ 3.15 + $ 1.50	$ 2.27 + $ 2.73

Sentence Busters › Rewrite these sentences so that they are correct.

1. i do believe you are write

_____

2. no i do not like that show

_____

⟨ ANALOGY of the Day ⟩

Ski is to **snow** as **ice-skate** is to _____.

WORD of the Day   Use the word in a sentence.

dim: slightly dark; hard to see

_____

_____

THINK TANK

Jane's plant grew 2 inches, Ralph's plant grew 3 inches, and Thad's plant grew $2\frac{1}{2}$ inches.

How much did their plants grow in all?

Answer: _____

Splash into Handwriting

plant

inches

grew

equal

angles

Brainteaser

Draw a shape with five sides.	Draw a shape with three equal sides.	Draw a shape with four angles.

Skill-Building Morning Jumpstarts   Scholastic Professional Books

Name _____ Date _____

✦Magic Number✦

The magic number is in the

_____ place.

ten-thousands	thousands	hundreds	tens	ones
9	0,	0	0	1

Expanded Form: _____

Words: _____

Math Busters

2 x 9 = ___   6 x 3 = ___   4 x 5 = ___

9 x 3 = ___   6 x 2 = ___   4 x 6 = ___

Sentence Busters Rewrite these sentences so that they are correct.

1. i saw two babys at the park

_____

2. sharon saw one ant three spiders and 4 ladybugs

_____

ANALOGY of the Day

Apple is to **red** as **banana** is to _____.

WORD of the Day   Use the word in a sentence.

cherish: to love and care about someone or something

_____

_____

THINK TANK

Maria ate 41 peas. Tom ate 31 peas.
Jerry ate 85 peas.

Who ate the most peas? _____   Who ate the fewest? _____

How many more peas did Jerry eat than Maria? _____

Splash into Handwriting

cherish

adore

love

peas

possible

Brainteaser

Matt, Al, and Bess sit together on
the bus. Fill in their names on the
lines to show all the different
possible seating arrangements.

Matt	Bess	Al	_____	_____	_____
Matt	Al	Bess	Bess	_____	_____
Al	_____	_____	_____	_____	_____

Skill-Building Morning Jumpstarts   Scholastic Professional Books

Name _____ Date _____

✦Magic Number✦

The magic number is in the

_____ place.

ten-thousands	thousands	hundreds	tens	ones
5	6,	6	4	9

Expanded Form: _____

Words: _____

Math Busters

12 inches = _____ foot

24 inches = _____ feet

$\frac{1}{2}$ foot = _____ inches

Sentence Busters Rewrite these sentences so that they are correct.

1. how many days are in the Month of january

_____

2. yesterday i tripped and chiped my tooth

_____

ANALOGY of the Day

A is to **V** as **F** is to _____ .

WORD of the Day   Use the word in a sentence.

advise: to give suggestions or advice

_____

_____

THINK TANK

Al was born 5 years before his little brother Jeff. Jeff was born in 1995. When was Al born?

Answer: _____

Splash into Handwriting

today

tomorrow

yesterday

older

younger

Brainteaser

How old are you today? _____

How old will you be in 5 years? _____

How old will you be in 12 years? _____

How old will you be in the year 2020? _____

80

Name _____   Date _____

✦Magic Number✦

The magic number is in the

_____ place.

ten-thousands	thousands	hundreds	tens	ones
2	3,	4	5	6

Expanded Form: _____

Words: _____

Math Busters

665 − 223	749 − 568	887 − 473

Sentence Busters Rewrite these sentences so that they are correct.

1. i finally saw the movie about chickens

_____

2. Mandy exclaimed, "I got a new job

_____

ANALOGY of the Day

⬛ is to ⬜ as ◓ is to _____ .

WORD of the Day   Use the word in a sentence.

ability: skill

_____

_____

THINK TANK

Fill in the missing numbers on the number line.

$\frac{1}{2}$ 1 $1\frac{1}{2}$ $2\frac{1}{2}$ 4

Splash into Handwriting

half

halves

fourth

big

bigger

Brainteaser

Find and circle the following words:

ability

advise

dim

modern

rush

cause

A	B	I	L	I	T	Y
D	I	M	W	P	Y	L
V	B	O	V	C	P	C
I	O	D	L	A	B	H
S	M	E	S	U	D	U
E	R	R	U	S	H	O
E	S	N	N	E	P	F

Name _____ Date _____

✦ Magic Number ✦

The magic number is in the

_____ place.

ten-thousands	thousands	hundreds	tens	ones
	7,	4	2	3

Expanded Form: _____

Words: _____

Math Busters

4 x 4 = ___   6 x 6 = ___   8 x 8 = ___

5 x 5 = ___   7 x 7 = ___   9 x 9 = ___

Sentence Busters Rewrite these sentences so that they are correct.

1. i like you very much shouted demetrius

_____

2. our firend charles is in that Class

_____

ANALOGY of the Day

Modern is to **new** as **ancient** is to _____ .

WORD of the Day Use the word in a sentence.

celebrity: a famous person, such as a movie star

_____

THINK TANK

Debbie scored 22 points in the basketball game. Each basket she scored was worth 2 points. How many baskets did she make?

Answer: _____

Splash into Handwriting

basketball

points

score

modern

ancient

Brainteaser

On Friday, Nate ran a mile in 6 minutes. On Monday, Nate ran a mile in 5 minutes and 35 seconds. How much longer did it take Nate to run a mile on Friday than on Monday?

Answer: _____

Skill-Building Morning Jumpstarts   Scholastic Professional Books

Name _____ Date _____

☆Magic Number☆

The magic number is in the

_____ place.

ten-thousands	thousands	hundreds	tens	ones
3	7,	3	0	0

Expanded Form: _____

Words: _____

Math Busters

3 feet = _____ yard

_____ feet = 2 yards

9 feet = _____ yards

Sentence Busters · Rewrite these sentences so that they are correct.

1. how many foot are in a yard

_____

2. wood you like to answer the question

_____

ANALOGY of the Day

West is to **east** as **north** is to _____.

WORD of the Day   Use the word in a sentence.

discover: to find or find out

_____

_____

THINK TANK

Fill in the bar graph using the data below.

12 butterflies

9 dogs

5 rabbits

7 frogs

Splash into Handwriting

discover

butterflies

rabbits

frogs

dogs

Brainteaser

Create a new money system using sweets.
Draw a kind of candy or dessert that you
would use for each of these types of money.
The first one has been filled in.

penny =   nickel =   dime =   quarter =   dollar bill =

How can you show $1.17 in candy? _____

86

Name _____   Date _____

Magic Number

The magic number is in the

_____ place.

ten-thousands	thousands	hundreds	tens	ones
		3	0	8

Expanded Form: _____

Words: _____

Math Busters

What number is 10 more than 2,987?	What number is 100 less than 2,987?	What number is 100 more than 2,987?
_____	_____	_____

Sentence Busters Rewrite these sentences so that they are correct.

1. i would like to meat the new Principal

_____

2. i expect great things from you said ms shearin

_____

ANALOGY of the Day

Butterfly is to **chrysalis** as **chick** is to _____ .

WORD of the Day Use the word in a sentence.

purpose: the reason for doing something; goal

_____

_____

THINK TANK

(2, D) marks the house.

(5, A) marks a patch of quicksand.

The treasure is buried at (3, B).
Draw an X to mark the spot.

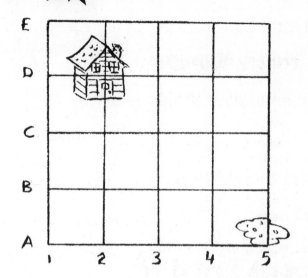

Splash into Handwriting

treasure

grid

pair

forward

backward

Brainteaser

Can you think of five words
that are spelled the same
forward and backward?
Write them on the lines.
(Example: *pop*)

Skill-Building Morning Jumpstarts   Scholastic Professional Books

Name _____ Date _____

✨ Magic Number ✨

The magic number is in the

_____ place.

ten-thousands	thousands	hundreds	tens	ones
	4,	3	**8**	7

Expanded Form: _____

Words: _____

Math Busters

5 x 8 = _____   6 x 6 = _____   4 x 9 = _____

6 x 8 = _____   7 x 6 = _____   5 x 9 = _____

Sentence Busters — Rewrite these sentences so that they are correct.

1. we will study about mexico and canada

_____

2. she new all about the Countries and Continents

_____

ANALOGY of the Day

Oak is to **tree** as **rose** is to _____.

WORD of the Day — Use the word in a sentence.

custom: a tradition

_____

_____

THINK TANK

Think of five animals. Then write their names in order from smallest animal to largest animal.

_____

_____

_____

_____

_____

Splash into Handwriting

Mexico

Canada

custom

smallest

largest

Brainteaser

Draw an imaginary creature and give it a name. Then write five adjectives that describe this creature.

_____

_____

_____

_____

Animal's name: _____

Skill-Building Morning Jumpstarts   Scholastic Professional Books

Name _____ Date _____

✦Magic Number✦

The magic number is in the

_____ place.

ten-thousands	thousands	hundreds	tens	ones
			9	7

Expanded Form: _____

Words: _____

Math Busters

One hour later than

9:00 A.M. is _____.

Two hours before

3:00 P.M. is _____.

Three hours later than

12:00 noon is _____.

Sentence Busters Rewrite these sentences so that they are correct.

1. I have blue yellow green and pink paint

_____

2. nora would like to go on the saleboat

_____

ANALOGY of the Day

Uncle is to **nephew** as **aunt** is to _____.

WORD of the Day   Use the word in a sentence.

mystery: something that is puzzling and needs to be solved

_____

_____

THINK TANK

There are 31 students in the juggling club that meets after school. Eighteen members are girls. How many members are boys?

Answer: _____

Splash into Handwriting

mystery

puzzle

solve

uncle

aunt

Brainteaser

If you could make an after-school club, what would it be about? Create a fun title for you new club.
Design a T-shirt, too!

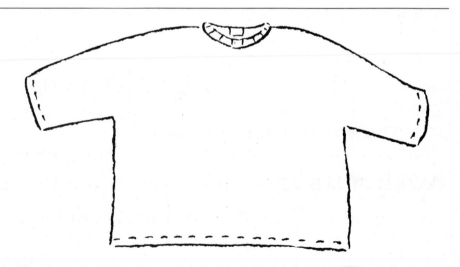

Club title: _____

Skill-Building Morning Jumpstarts Scholastic Professional Books

Name _____ Date _____

✫ Magic Number ✫

The magic number is in the

_____ place.

ten-thousands	thousands	hundreds	tens	ones
	9,4	3		6

Expanded Form: _____

Words: _____

Math Busters   What fraction is shaded?

_____   _____   _____

Sentence Busters Rewrite these sentences so that they are correct.

1. miss poston bought a present for her freind

_____

2. mrs ortiz replied, "i am so excited to be here

_____

ANALOGY of the Day

North is to **south** as **west** is to _____.

WORD of the Day   Use the word in a sentence.

depart: to leave

_____

_____

THINK TANK

The child's temperature was 98°F. The temperature on the thermometer outside showed 90°F. How much warmer was the child's temperature than the temperature outside?

Answer: _____

Splash into Handwriting

reply

replied

temperature

thermometer

degrees

Brainteaser

Draw the line of symmetry in each of these pictures. The first one has been done for you.

Skill-Building Morning Jumpstarts   Scholastic Professional Books

JUMPSTART 45

Side A

Name ______________________________ Date ________________

Magic Number

ten-thousands	thousands	hundreds	tens	ones
3	7,	8	**8**	7

The magic number is in the

____________________ place.

Expanded Form: ______________________________

Words: ______________________________

Math Busters

Robert stopped reading at 3:30 P.M. He read for 2 hours. What time did he start reading? Draw the clock hands.

stop

start

Sentence Busters

Rewrite these sentences so that they are correct.

1. canada is north of the united states of America

____

2. wow exclaimed mr gunter

____

ANALOGY of the Day

Canada is to **country** as **North America** is to ________________.

WORD of the Day

Use the word in a sentence.

fragile: easily broken; delicate

____

____

THINK TANK

If one side of the square picture frame measures 6 inches, how many inches does the frame measure all the way around? (All sides of the frame are equal in length.)

Answer: _____

Splash into Handwriting

fragile

delicate

count

record

information

Brainteaser

Count the number of chairs, desks, and people in your classroom. Record the information on the bar graph.

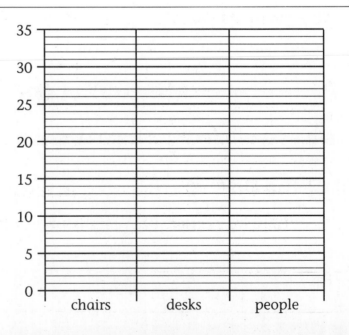

Skill-Building Morning Jumpstarts Scholastic Professional Books

Name _____ Date _____

✧Magic Number✧

The magic number is in the

_____ place.

ten-thousands	thousands	hundreds	tens	ones
5	2,	9	0	9

Expanded Form: _____

Words: _____

Math Busters

Shade to show each fraction.

$\dfrac{1}{4}$ $\qquad\qquad$ $\dfrac{1}{3}$ $\qquad\qquad$ $\dfrac{1}{2}$

Sentence Busters

Rewrite these sentences so that they are correct.

1. today is november 3 2002

_____

2. have you ever scene a canada goose

_____

ANALOGY of the Day

Salad is to **fork** as **soup** is to _____.

WORD of the Day

Use the word in a sentence.

liquid: something that is wet and can be poured

_____

THINK TANK

Eileen had 2 cups of lemonade in a pitcher. She poured $\frac{1}{2}$ cup in one glass and $\frac{1}{2}$ cup in another glass. How much did she have left in the pitcher?

Answer: _____

Splash into Handwriting

fraction

shade

popcorn

liquid

poured

Brainteaser

You are going to the movies, and you have $8.00 to spend. How will you spend the money to buy a ticket and a snack?

What did you buy? _____

_____

How much money did you spend? _____

How much money do you have left? _____

PRICE LIST	
Movie ticket	$5.00
Small popcorn	$1.00
Large popcorn	$2.00
Small soda	$0.50
Large soda	$1.00
Candy	$0.75

98

Name _____ Date _____

✦Magic Number✦

The magic number is in the

_____ place.

ten-thousands	thousands	hundreds	tens	ones
9	8,	6	6	5

Expanded Form: _____

Words: _____

Math Busters

13 × 2	22 × 4	11 × 3

Sentence Busters Rewrite these sentences so that they are correct.

1. what is the whether like in florida

_____

2. I went to lots of museum in new york city

_____

ANALOGY of the Day

Bakery is to **bread** as **butcher shop** is to _____.

WORD of the Day Use the word in a sentence.

absorb: to take in or soak up something, often a liquid

_____

_____

THINK TANK

How much money is shown? Write the amount in numbers and words. List one thing you could buy with this amount of money.

_____

_____

_____

Splash into Handwriting

absorb

New York

museum

value

worth

Brainteaser

If you could create your own museum, what would be in it? (Stickers? Skateboards? Your own artwork?) Draw a picture of your museum or a part of it. Give your museum a name.

Name _____ Date _____

✨Magic Number✨

The magic number is in the

_____ place.

ten-thousands	thousands	hundreds	tens	ones
9	7,	4	2	6

Expanded Form: _____

Words: _____

Math Busters

The movie starts at 7:00 P.M. It is now 6:00 P.M. How long until the movie starts?

Answer: _____

It is now 2:30 P.M. In 45 minutes the cookies will be finished baking. At what time will the cookies be done?

Answer: _____

Sentence Busters ⟩ Rewrite these sentences so that they are correct.

1. we wanted to buy plates balloons and streamers for hour party

_____

2. my watch tells time it has a alarm

_____

ANALOGY of the Day

Cream cheese is to **bagel** as **frosting** is to _____ .

WORD of the Day   Use the word in a sentence.

summary: a brief statement that tells the main idea

_____

THINK TANK

Katherine found 58 pretty seashells on the beach. On the way home, 34 shells broke and she threw them out. Then Sally gave Katherine 8 more shells. How many shells does Katherine have in all?

Answer: _____

Splash into Handwriting

Katherine

beach

beaches

seashells

ocean

Brainteaser

Two boats left the dock at the same time. One boat arrived at an island in 55 minutes. The other boat arrived at the same island in 1 hour and 7 minutes. How much longer did it take the second boat to travel?

Answer: _____

Skill-Building Morning Jumpstarts   Scholastic Professional Books

Name _____ Date _____

☆Magic Number☆

The magic number is in the

_____ place.

ten-thousands	thousands	hundreds	tens	ones
9,	**0**	**0**	**2**	

Expanded Form: _____

Words: _____

Math Busters

1 year = _____ months

1 year = _____ days

$\frac{1}{2}$ year = _____ months

Sentence Busters Rewrite these sentences so that they are correct.

1. 3 mans went to the store

_____

2. the view from the Mountain is beuatiful

_____

ANALOGY of the Day

Shovel is to **dig** as **knife** is to _____.

WORD of the Day   Use the word in a sentence.

fantasy: a story or thoughts that are imagined rather than real

_____

THINK TANK

Put these months of the year
in alphabetical order:

_____

September

_____

April

_____

February

_____

December

_____

July

_____

March

_____

Splash into Handwriting

fantasy

imagination

favorite

days

months

Brainteaser

What month of the year is your
favorite? Draw a picture of what
you like to do during that month.

Skill-Building Morning Jumpstarts Scholastic Professional Books

Name _____ Date _____

Magic Number

The magic number is in the

_____ place.

ten-thousands	thousands	hundreds	tens	ones
	6,	2	9	7

Expanded Form: _____

Words: _____

Math Busters

Shade to show each fraction.

$\frac{3}{4}$ $\frac{2}{3}$ $\frac{3}{10}$

Sentence Busters

Rewrite these sentences so that they are correct.

1. october is the tenth month of the year

_____

2. my family gets together for thanksgiving in november

_____

ANALOGY of the Day

Elephant is to **big** as **mouse** is to _____.

WORD of the Day

Use the word in a sentence.

sparkle: to glitter or shine with flashes of light

_____

THINK TANK

Terri planted 150 flower seeds in her garden. Only 78 of them grew into flowers. How many of the seeds did not grow?

Answer: _____

Splash into Handwriting

garden

flowers

seeds

sparkle

glitter

Brainteaser

Write a rap with the word **snap** in it.

Skill-Building Morning Jumpstarts Scholastic Professional Books

Answer Key

Jumpstart 1
Magic Number: The magic number is in the tens place; 500 + 70 + 7; five hundred seventy-seven
Math Busters: 1:15; 5:30; 9:45
Sentence Busters: (Answers will vary. Sample sentences are provided for all Sentence Busters.) **1.** Today we will learn about numbers.
2. Do you have a pet shark?
Analogy of the Day: Smell is to nose as see is to **eyes** (or **eye**).
Word of the Day: (Answers will vary. Sample sentences are provided for each Word of the Day.) The painting is one of the artist's greatest **masterpieces**.
Think Tank: The clowns have 33 buttons in all.
Brainteaser: There are nine triangles in the picture. (Note: Some triangles overlap.)

Jumpstart 2
Magic Number: The magic number is in the ones place; 400 + 80 + 6; four hundred eighty-six
Math Busters: 1, 2, <u>3</u>, <u>4</u>, 5; 56, <u>57</u>, 58, <u>59</u>, 60; 25, 24, <u>23</u>, 22, <u>21</u>
Sentence Busters: **1.** How many days are in a week?
2. Sally, Jeff, and Ashley went to the zoo. (Note: The comma after *Jeff* is optional.)
Analogy of the Day: △ is to ○ as ▲ is to ●.
Word of the Day: The ground is still **moist** from the rain yesterday.
Think Tank: You have 5 muffins left.
Brainteaser: Answers will vary.

Jumpstart 3
Magic Number: The magic number is in the hundreds place; 7,000 + 800 + 90; seven thousand eight hundred ninety
Math Busters: 5 + 4 = 9; 3 + 4 = 7; 9 − 3 = 6; 6 + 5 = 11; 7 + 5 = 12; 8 − 5 = 3
Sentence Busters: **1.** Yes, the book is in the library.
2. <u>Charlotte's Web</u> is a great book.
Analogy of the Day: Drink is to thirsty as eat is to **hungry**.
Word of the Day: The teacher thought it was **peculiar** when her students asked for more homework.
Think Tank: Karen sold the fewest tickets.
Brainteaser: Answers will vary.

Jumpstart 4
Magic Number: The magic number is in the thousands place; 20,000 + 4,000 + 600 + 80 + 9; twenty-four thousand six hundred eighty-nine
Math Busters: 7 − 4 = 3; 3 + 6 = 9; 8 − 4 = 4; 6 − 4 = 2; 8 + 9 = 17; 9 − 2 = 7
Sentence Busters: **1.** We go to the movies after school on Thursday. **2.** Jerry loves broccoli, spinach, and carrots. (Note: The comma after *spinach* is optional.)
Analogy of the Day: Lemon is to sour as sugar is to **sweet**.
Word of the Day: I stirred the ingredients in a bowl to **combine** them.
Think Tank: Friday, Monday, Saturday, Sunday, Thursday, Tuesday, Wednesday
Brainteaser: rTsydhau = Thursday; Fydari = Friday

Jumpstart 5
Magic Number: The magic number is in the thousands place; 1,000 + 100 + 70 + 5; one thousand one hundred seventy-five
Math Busters: 254 (even); 1,230 (even); 3,745 (odd)
Sentence Busters: **1.** Dan, can you name the oceans?
2. The Atlantic Ocean is a large body of water.
Analogy of the Day: A is to a as B is to **b**.
Word of the Day: Cold is an **antonym** for hot.

Think Tank: Answers will vary. These are possible answers: high, low; on, off; slow, fast; early, late; old, young.
Brainteaser: Answers will vary. These are possible answers: long, tray, fang, beep.

Jumpstart 6
Magic Number: The magic number is in the tens place; 300 + 50 + 7; three hundred fifty-seven
Math Busters: 5 + 5 = 10; 6 + 6 = 12; 5 + 5 + 5 = 15; 6 + 6 + 6 = 18; 5 + 5 + 5 + 5 + 5 = 25; 6 + 6 + 6 + 6 = 24
Sentence Busters: **1.** The boy was sitting on the grass.
2. I will give the present to Patrick.
Analogy of the Day: Foot is to toes as hand is to **fingers**.
Word of the Day: We arranged the beads in a colorful **pattern**.
Think Tank: She spent $5.00 in all.
Brainteaser:

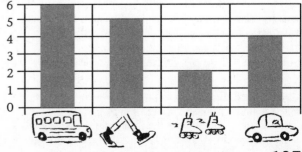

Jumpstart 7
Magic Number: The magic number is in the hundreds place; 200 + 80 + 5; two hundred eighty-five
Math Busters: 4:00; 12:15; 9:00
Sentence Busters: **1.** Katy will go to the store.
2. Do you want to go with her?
Analogy of the Day: ○ is to ● as is to   .
Word of the Day: After a **brief** rainstorm, it was sunny for the rest of the day.
Think Tank: There are two children behind Al.
Brainteaser: See drawing at right.

Jumpstart 8
Magic Number: The magic number is in the tens place; 10 + 9; nineteen
Math Busters: 199; 201; 300
Sentence Busters: **1.** Jim went to the store to get apples, oranges, and a banana. (Note: The comma after *oranges* is optional.)
2. When will we get to go outside for recess?
Analogy of the Day: Sandals are to summer as boots are to **winter**.
Word of the Day: Juan looked at the basketball in order to draw a **sphere**.
Think Tank: Answers will vary. These are possible answers: basketball, soccer ball, globe, orange, baseball, bubble, marble.
Brainteaser: Answers will vary.

Jumpstart 9
Magic Number: The magic number is in the ones place; 6,000 + 500 + 70 + 8; six thousand five hundred seventy-eight
Math Busters: 2, <u>4</u>, 6, 8, <u>10</u>, 12; 3, 5, <u>7</u>, 9, <u>11</u>, 13; 22, <u>24</u>, 26, 28, <u>30</u>, 32
Sentence Busters: **1.** We will go to see Mrs. Jefferson today.
2. Did you read the book <u>Green Eggs and Ham</u>?
Analogy of the Day: Square is to cube as circle is to **sphere**.
Word of the Day: Will's **grief** lasted for several weeks after his best friend moved away.
Think Tank:

Brainteaser: Answers will vary. These are possible answers: cat, tan, on, ton, aim, man, tin, can, Tom, mat, not, union, onion.

Jumpstart 10

Magic Number: The magic number is in the hundreds place; 8,000 + 300 + 60 + 7; eight thousand three hundred sixty-seven

Math Busters: 1, 4, 7, <u>10</u>, <u>13</u>, 16; 5, 10, <u>15</u>, <u>20</u>, 25, 30; 101, 102, <u>103</u>, <u>104</u>, 105

Sentence Busters: 1. Today I will eat at my Aunt Judy's house. **2.** Tomorrow I will eat at home.

Analogy of the Day: Back is to front as left is to **right**.

Word of the Day: I prefer to read **fiction** because I like imaginative stories.

Think Tank: There are 7 boys in front of Bobby and 20 boys behind him.

Brainteaser: Answers will vary.

Jumpstart 11

Magic Number: The magic number is in the thousands place; 2,000 + 100 + 30 + 9; two thousand one hundred thirty-nine

Math Busters: 4 or 5; 10 or 11; 101, 102, 103, 104, 105, 106, 107, 108, or 109

Sentence Busters: 1. Mr. Johnson reads five newspapers every day. **2.** Have you seen my new book?

Analogy of the Day: ▮ is to ▯ as ◐ is to ◑.

Word of the Day: After a **temporary** delay, the traffic began to move again.

Think Tank: Lisa has $1.50 left in all.

Brainteaser: Answers will vary. These are possible answers: cat, bat, rat, fat, mat, sat, that, chat, vat, at, brat, pat.

Jumpstart 12

Magic Number: The magic number is in the thousands place; 3,000 + 400 + 40 + 6; three thousand four hundred forty-six

Math Busters: 50 cents; 15 cents; 12 cents

Sentence Busters: 1. The dog barks at the cat. **2.** The cat is jumping on the chair.

Analogy of the Day: AA BB is to Aa Bb as FF GG is to **Ff Gg**.

Word of the Day: Fearful is a **synonym** for afraid.

Think Tank: Answers will vary. These are possible answers: neat = tidy; messy = sloppy; tired = sleepy.

Brainteaser: Answers will vary.

Jumpstart 13

Magic Number: The magic number is in the hundreds place; 7,000 + 100 + 50 + 6; seven thousand one hundred fifty-six

Math Busters: 12 + 13 = 25; 10 + 30 = 40; 11 + 21 = 32

Sentence Busters: 1. Many people like to go to the movies. **2.** The clown knows how to juggle.

Analogy of the Day: Bird is to fly as fish is to **swim**.

Word of the Day: I will **remain** inside today because it is raining.

Think Tank: octagon ○; square □; hexagon ○; rectangle ▭

Brainteaser: Answers will vary.

Jumpstart 14

Magic Number: The magic number is in the hundreds place; 500 + 40 + 3; five hundred forty-three

Math Busters: 2,546 (even); 7,961 (odd); 3,450 (even)

Sentence Busters: 1. The girl is working on a clay pot. **2.** How many pots has Billy made?

Analogy of the Day: Apple is to fruit as potato is to **vegetable**.

Word of the Day: The Atlantic Ocean is **vast**.

Think Tank: They found 15 different Web sites in all.

Brainteaser: Answers will vary. These are possible answers: Vast—oceans, countries, sky; Tiny—ants, dust, sprinkles.

Jumpstart 15

Magic Number: The magic number is in the ones place; 3,000 + 400 + 50 + 9; three thousand four hundred fifty-nine

Math Busters: 26 + 13 = 39; 41 + 52 = 93; 74 + 25 = 99

Sentence Busters: 1. Did Ramon eat any grapes today? **2.** Megan put nine cookies on a tray.

Analogy of the Day: Sun is to day as moon is to **night**.

Word of the Day: The scientist used a microscope to **examine** the cell.

Think Tank: Answers will vary.

Brainteaser: Answers will vary. These are possible answers: jump, smile, balance, leap, move, spill.

Jumpstart 16

Magic Number: The magic number is in the hundreds place; 500 + 60 + 7; five hundred sixty-seven

Math Busters: 57 + 28 = 85 ; 29 + 91 = 120; 78 + 33 = 111

Sentence Busters: 1. Does Peter have books? **2.** Yes, Peter has four books.

Analogy of the Day: Sheep is to lamb as dog is to **puppy**.

Word of the Day: I have never seen such a **unique** ring.

Think Tank: There are 10 people in between Jared and Gwen.

Brainteaser: Answers will vary. These are possible answers: vest, gate, ate, eat, set, invest, nest, test, ten, tin, tag, age, tan, van, gain.

Jumpstart 17

Magic Number: The magic number is in the thousands place; 5,000 + 600 + 70; five thousand six hundred seventy

Math Busters: 38 – 5 = 33; 49 – 11 = 38; 52 – 12 = 40

Sentence Busters: 1. Can the girls run in the race tomorrow? **2.** The girls can run in the race on Friday.

Analogy of the Day: ⇄ is to ⇆ as ↑↑ is to ↓↓.

Word of the Day: I watched the clouds **vanish** as the sun came out.

Think Tank: The greatest possible number is 8,742; the smallest possible number is 2,478; a number with a 2 in the tens place is 4,728 (answers will vary).

Brainteaser:

```
E E G R I E F U
E X R E M A I N
Y B A V M F M I
A W E M O X N Q
E E B R I E F U
Q H C P S N N E
U V A S T T E W
```

Jumpstart 18

Magic Number: The magic number is in the thousands place; 4,000 + 500 + 80 + 7; four thousand five hundred eighty-seven

Math Busters: Answers will vary. These are possible answers: 44; 549; 4,896.

Sentence Busters: 1. A horse was running quickly in the meadow. **2.** Did the horse run quickly in the meadow?

Analogy of the Day: Month is to year as day is to **week**.

Word of the Day: I would like to **invent** a machine that does my homework.

Think Tank: Answers will vary. These are possible answers: their, they're, there; see, sea; be, bee; sail, sale; fare, fair; ate, eight.

Brainteaser: Answers will vary.

Jumpstart 19

Magic Number: The magic number is in the tens place; 600 + 60 + 7; six hundred sixty-seven

Math Busters: 25 – 13 = 12; 46 – 21 = 25; 59 – 35 = 24

Sentence Busters: 1. I read a book called <u>Arthur's Eyes</u>. **2.** Have you read a book that has chapters?

Analogy of the Day: Girl is to boy as woman is to **man**.

Word of the Day: The Pilgrims packed a lot of food for their **voyage**.

Think Tank: Twelve children went to the party.

Brainteaser: You will need 40 cookies and 20 fruit cups.

Jumpstart 20

Magic Number: The magic number is in the ten-thousands place; 40,000 + 6,000 + 100 + 70; forty-six thousand one hundred seventy

Math Busters: 32 > 28; 54 < 63; 1,008 = 1,008

Sentence Busters: 1. I like swimming, basketball, and tennis. (Note: The comma after *basketball* is optional.)
2. I told you that I would save you a seat.

Analogy of the Day: Toothbrush is to teeth as hairbrush is to **hair**.

Word of the Day: Ben could not wait to ride the Ferris wheel at the **carnival**.

Think Tank: She has 9 books left.

Brainteaser: Answers will vary.

Jumpstart 21

Magic Number: The magic number is in the thousands place; 20,000 + 400 + 30 + 5; twenty thousand four hundred thirty-five

Math Busters: 98 > 78; 64 > 44; 23 < 54

Sentence Busters: 1. Sam has on new shoes today.
2. Maya can't wait to go on the field trip.

Analogy of the Day: Leopard is to spots as zebra is to **stripes**.

Word of the Day: The trapeze artists will **amaze** the audience with their daring tricks.

Think Tank:

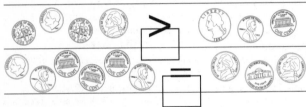

Brainteaser: Answers will vary.

Jumpstart 22

Magic Number: The magic number is in the ones place; 1,000 + 300 + 50; one thousand three hundred fifty

Math Busters: 85 − 62 = 23; 74 − 65 = 9; 97 − 35 = 62

Sentence Busters: 1. What is the name of your school?
2. We don't want to play outside.

Analogy of the Day: Snake is to slither as frog is to **hop**.

Word of the Day: The side of a pyramid is shaped like a **triangle**.

Think Tank: (top to bottom) Gadget, Chuckles, Toto, Ralph

Brainteaser: Answers will vary. These are possible answers: apple, award, amaze, alphabet, Arizona, artist, afraid.

Jumpstart 23

Magic Number: The magic number is in the tens place; 10,000 + 2,000 + 400 + 80 + 7; twelve thousand four hundred eighty-seven

Math Busters: 37 + 67 = 104; 92 − 58 = 34; 84 + 21 = 105

Sentence Busters: 1. "Why is the sky blue?" asked Eddie.
2. "Where are you going?" asked Terry.

Analogy of the Day: Cow is to calf as cat is to **kitten**.

Word of the Day: We found an **ancient** fossil in the desert.

Think Tank: Ronald had 5 peanuts left.

Brainteaser: Answers will vary. These are possible answers.

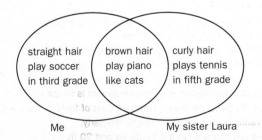

Jumpstart 24

Magic Number: The magic number is in the hundreds place; 8,000 + 400 + 40 + 3; eight thousand four hundred forty-three

Math Busters:

25 cents   28 cents   40 cents

Sentence Busters: 1. "When will he bake the cake?" I asked.
2. Luis will bake a cake on Wednesday.

Analogy of the Day: Loud is to quiet as high is to **low**.

Word of the Day: The cafeteria serves a **variety** of foods so that there is something for everyone.

Think Tank: I will have $7.50 left.

Brainteaser: Answers will vary. These are possible answers: form, inform, mat, man, motion, formation, rim, rat, arm, nation, fan, ran.

Jumpstart 25

Magic Number: The magic number is in the ten-thousands place; 30,000 + 3,000 + 300 + 30 + 1; thirty-three thousand three hundred thirty-one

Math Busters: 178 + 36 = 214; 287 + 158 = 445; 708 + 249 = 957

Sentence Busters: 1. "Today is Thursday," said Miss Johnson.
2. It will take two minutes to walk to the park.

Analogy of the Day: Bird is to nest as spider is to **web**.

Word of the Day: He was amazed to find such an **uncommon** rock in the yard.

Think Tank:

Brainteaser: Answers will vary. These are possible answers: hip, lip, flip, tip, whip, nip, drip, rip, zip, sip, dip.

Jumpstart 26

Magic Number: The magic number is in the hundreds place; 6,000 + 100 + 40 + 7; six thousand one hundred forty-seven

Math Busters: She finished at 1:00 P.M.

Sentence Busters: 1. The boys are named John, James, Joe, and Jack. (Note: The comma after *Joe* is optional.)
2. Did you eat at the restaurant today?

Analogy of the Day: Asleep is to night as awake is to **day**.

Word of the Day: Our math teacher asked us to write both the **numeral** and the word for each number.

Think Tank: I can buy six books.

Brainteaser: Answers will vary. These are possible answers: People—teacher, students; Places—writing center, classroom library, closet; Things—desks, chalkboard, pencils.

Jumpstart 27

Magic Number: The magic number is in the tens place; 90 + 7; ninety-seven

Math Busters: 33 + 22 + 11 = 66 ; 45 + 23 + 61 = 129; 24 + 56 + 87 = 167

Sentence Busters: 1. You're a terrific friend, Rebecca.
2. Did you check your work?

Analogy of the Day: Hear is to ears as smell is to **nose**.

Word of the Day: The **timid** kitten hid under the bed all day.

Think Tank: cube ⬡ ; cylinder ▢ ; cone ▽ ; pyramid △

Brainteaser: Answers will vary.

Jumpstart 28

Magic Number: The magic number is in the ones place; 2,000 + 500 + 90 + 2; two thousand five hundred ninety-two

Math Busters: 313 – 21 = 292; 438 – 218 = 220; 879 – 455 = 424

Sentence Busters: 1. There are five cats and five dogs in their yard. **2.** Their Aunt Sarah is coming over for dinner.

Analogy of the Day: Smell is to odor as hear is to **sound**.

Word of the Day: We drove over the bridge to reach the **island**.

Think Tank: Frank is the shortest.

Brainteaser: Answers will vary. These are possible answers.

I am a **monkey**. (kind of animal)

I am **furry**, **cute**, and **energetic**. (adjectives)

I like to **eat**, **climb**, and **play**. (verbs)

and I can **swing** from trees! (verb)

Jumpstart 29

Magic Number: The magic number is in the ones place; 100 + 90; one hundred ninety

Math Busters: 85 cents; 75 cents

Sentence Busters: 1. Rita ordered a grilled cheese sandwich. **2.** She also ordered dessert.

Analogy of the Day: Snake is to scales as bird is to **feathers**.

Word of the Day: What was the **cause** of the argument?

Think Tank:

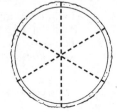

Brainteaser: They would all enjoy onions and pepperoni.

Jumpstart 30

Magic Number: The magic number is in the hundreds place; 100 + 40 + 2; one hundred forty-two

Math Busters: 384 + 256 = 640; 667 – 446 = 221; 851 – 197 = 654

Sentence Busters: 1. Ms. Smith fell on Mr. Johnson's foot. **2.** Mr. Johnson's toe hurt a lot.

Analogy of the Day: Cat is to meow as dog is to **bark**.

Word of the Day: Every day, the children **rush** to the playground.

Think Tank: 5 days were snowy. 2 days were rainy. There were 3 more snowy days than rainy days.

Brainteaser: Answers will vary. These are possible answers: Loud noise—helicopters, fireworks, alarms, horns; Quiet—bees, watch, refrigerator, heart

Jumpstart 31

Magic Number: The magic number is in the hundreds place; 80,000 + 8,000 + 200 + 40 + 8; eighty-eight thousand two hundred forty-eight

Math Busters: 7:30; 4:30; 9:45

Sentence Busters: 1. Are Lucy, Mary, and Kim friends? (Note: The comma after *Mary* is optional.) **2.** My friend Kendall is in third grade.

Analogy of the Day: Mother is to father as grandmother is to **grandfather**.

Word of the Day: Please **analyze** this problem and help me solve it.

Think Tank: $\frac{1}{4}$ of the pizza has pepperoni. $\frac{3}{4}$ of the pizza does not have pepperoni.

Brainteaser: 4 cups flour; 2 cups sugar; 6 tablespoons honey; 1 teaspoon salt; 10 tablespoons butter; $\frac{2}{3}$ cup raisins

Jumpstart 32

Magic Number: The magic number is in the ten-thousands place; 60,000 + 700 + 70 + 1; sixty thousand seven hundred seventy-one

Math Busters: 2 x 2 = 4; 4 x 2 = 8; 5 x 2 = 10; 3 x 3 = 9; 4 x 3 = 12; 5 x 3 = 15

Sentence Busters: 1. "Today is my birthday!" I shouted.

2. My dog Max is black and white.

Analogy of the Day: Fur is to dogs as feathers are to **birds**.

Word of the Day: The antique furniture looked out of place in the **modern** home.

Think Tank: We used 18 chocolate chips in all.

Brainteaser: Answers will vary. These are possible answers.

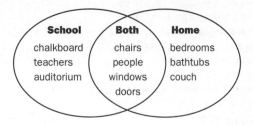

Jumpstart 33

Magic Number: The magic number is in the hundreds place; 1,000 + 800 + 70 + 2; one thousand eight hundred seventy-two

Math Busters: $1.50 + $.50 = $2.00; $2.00 + $.75 = $2.75; $1.25 + $2.25 = $3.50

Sentence Busters: 1. My cats Morris and Sydney are sweet and playful. **2.** Last year my family went to Williamsburg, Virginia.

Analogy of the Day: ○△ is to ●△ as □○ is to ■○.

Word of the Day: Will you please **explain** your answer so that everyone understands it?

Think Tank: They will have to pay $6.35 in total.

Brainteaser:

Jumpstart 34

Magic Number: The magic number is in the ten-thousands place; 40,000 + 4,000 + 900 + 10 + 8; forty-four thousand nine hundred eighteen

Math Busters:

Sentence Busters: 1. I hope our teacher feels better tomorrow. **2.** It's a great day to go to the park.

Analogy of the Day: ▲ is to ▼ as ◀ is to ▶.

Word of the Day: The storm caused the shack to **collapse**.

Think Tank: You spent six hours at school.

Brainteaser: Answers will vary.

Jumpstart 35

Magic Number: The magic number is in the ones place; 70,000 + 9,000 + 800 + 10 + 7; seventy-nine thousand eight hundred seventeen

Math Busters: $1.00 + $2.10 = $3.10; $3.15 + $1.50 = $4.65; $2.27 + $2.73 = $5.00

Sentence Busters: 1. I do believe you are right. **2.** No, I do not like that show.

Analogy of the Day: Ski is to snow as ice-skate is to **ice**.

Word of the Day: We could barely see anything in the **dim** cave.

Think Tank: Their plants grew seven and a half inches in all.

Brainteaser: Answers will vary. These are possible answers:

Jumpstart 36

Magic Number: The magic number is in the thousands place; 90,000 + 1; ninety thousand one

Math Busters: 2 x 9 = 18; 6 x 3 = 18; 4 x 5 = 20; 9 x 3 = 27; 6 x 2 = 12; 4 x 6 = 24

Sentence Busters: 1. I saw two babies at the park.
2. Sharon saw one ant, three spiders, and four ladybugs. (Note: The comma after *spiders* is optional.)

Analogy of the Day: Apple is to red as banana is to **yellow**.

Word of the Day: We all **cherish** our baby cousin.

Think Tank: Jerry ate the most peas. Tom ate the fewest peas. Jerry ate 44 more peas than Maria.

Brainteaser: Matt, Bess, Al; Matt, Al, Bess; Al, Bess, Matt; Al, Matt, Bess; Bess, Matt, Al; Bess, Al, Matt

Jumpstart 37

Magic Number: The magic number is in the ten-thousands place; 50,000 + 6,000 + 600 + 40 + 9; fifty-six thousand six hundred forty-nine

Math Busters: 12 inches = 1 foot; 24 inches = 2 feet; $\frac{1}{2}$ foot = 6 inches

Sentence Busters: 1. How many days are in the month of January?
2. Yesterday I tripped and chipped my tooth.

Analogy of the Day: A is to ∀ as F is to ꟻ.

Word of the Day: Maggie asked her grandmother to **advise** her about her problem.

Think Tank: Al was born in 1990.

Brainteaser: Answers will vary.

Jumpstart 38

Magic Number: The magic number is in the thousands place; 20,000 + 3,000 + 400 + 50 + 6; twenty-three thousand four hundred fifty-six

Math Busters: 665 – 223 = 442; 749 – 568 = 181; 887 – 473 = 414

Sentence Busters: 1. I finally saw the movie about chickens.
2. Mandy exclaimed, "I got a new job!"

Analogy of the Day: ▭ is to ▬ as ◖ is to ◐.

Word of the Day: His **ability** to run and juggle at the same time was amazing.

Think Tank: $\frac{1}{2}$, 1, $1\frac{1}{2}$, 2, $2\frac{1}{2}$, 3, $3\frac{1}{2}$, 4

Brainteaser:

A	B	I	L	I	T	Y
D	I	M	W	P	Y	L
V	B	O	V	C	P	C
I	O	D	L	A	B	H
S	M	E	S	U	D	U
E	R	R	U	S	H	O
E	S	N	N	E	P	F

Jumpstart 39

Magic Number: The magic number is in the thousands place; 7,000 + 400 + 20 + 3; seven thousand four hundred twenty-three

Math Busters: 4 x 4 = 16; 6 x 6 = 36; 8 x 8 = 64; 5 x 5 = 25; 7 x 7 = 49; 9 x 9 = 81

Sentence Busters: 1. "I like you very much!" shouted Demetrius.
2. Our friend Charles is in that class.

Analogy of the Day: Modern is to new as ancient is to **old**.

Word of the Day: The photographer followed the **celebrity** around the city.

Think Tank: Debbie made 11 baskets.

Brainteaser: It took Nate 25 more seconds to run a mile on Friday than on Monday.

Jumpstart 40

Magic Number: The magic number is in the ten-thousands place; 30,000 + 7,000 + 300; thirty-seven thousand three hundred

Math Busters: 3 feet = 1 yard; 6 feet = 2 yards; 9 feet = 3 yards

Sentence Busters: 1. How many feet are in a yard?
2. Would you like to answer the question?

Analogy of the Day: West is to east as north is to **south**.

Word of the Day: Did you **discover** the secret cave?

Think Tank:

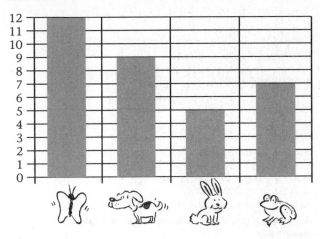

Brainteaser: Answers will vary. These are possible answers: penny = candy cane; nickel = cookie; dime = lollipop; quarter = cupcake; dollar bill = ice cream cone. You can show $1.17 with an ice cream cone, a lollipop, a cookie, and two candy canes.

Jumpstart 41

Magic Number: The magic number is in the ones place; 300 + 8; three hundred eight

Math Busters: 2,997; 2,887; 3,087

Sentence Busters: 1. I would like to meet the new principal.
2. "I expect great things from you," said Ms. Shearin.

Analogy of the Day: Butterfly is to chrysalis as chick is to **egg**.

Word of the Day: What is the **purpose** of this trip?

Think Tank:

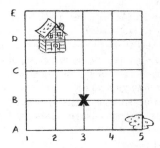

Brainteaser: Answers will vary. These are possible answers: mom, dad, sis, tot, wow, Bob.

Jumpstart 42

Magic Number: The magic number is in the tens place; 4,000 + 300 + 80 + 7; four thousand three hundred eighty-seven

Math Busters: 5 x 8 = 40; 6 x 6 = 36; 4 x 9 = 36; 6 x 8 = 48; 7 x 6 = 42; 5 x 9 = 45

Sentence Busters: 1. We will study about Mexico and Canada.
2. She knew all about the countries and continents.

Analogy of the Day: Oak is to tree as rose is to **flower**.

Word of the Day: It is a **custom** to sing songs during the holidays.

Think Tank: Answers will vary. There are possible answers: cat, wolf, pony, horse, elephant.

Brainteaser: Answers will vary.

Jumpstart 43

Magic Number: The magic number is in the tens place; 90 + 7; ninety-seven

Math Busters: One hour later than 9:00 a.m. is **10:00 A.M.**

Two hours before 3:00 P.M. is **1:00 P.M.**

Three hours later than 12:00 noon is **3:00** P.M.
Sentence Busters: 1. I have blue, yellow, green, and pink paint.
(Note: The comma after *green* is optional.)
2. Nora would like to go on the sailboat.
Analogy of the Day: Uncle is to nephew as aunt is to **niece**.
Word of the Day: The detective solved the **mystery** by studying all of the clues.
Think Tank: Thirteen members are boys.
Brainteaser: Answers will vary.

Jumpstart 44

Magic Number: The magic number is in the ones place;
9,000 + 400 + 30 + 6; nine thousand four hundred thirty-six
Math Busters: $\frac{1}{3}$; $\frac{5}{9}$; $\frac{3}{5}$
Sentence Busters: 1. Miss Poston bought a present for her friend.
2. Mrs. Ortiz replied, "I am so excited to be here!"
Analogy of the Day: North is to south as west is to **east**.
Word of the Day: We will **depart** for our trip at three o'clock.
Think Tank: The child's temperature was 8 degrees warmer than the temperature ouside.
Brainteaser: Answers will vary. These are possible answers.

Jumpstart 45

Magic Number: The magic number is in the tens place;
30,000 + 7,000 + 800 + 80 + 7; thirty-seven thousand eight hundred eighty-seven
Math Busters:

stop   start

Sentence Busters: 1. Canada is north of the United States of America. **2.** "Wow!" exclaimed Mr. Gunter.
Analogy of the Day: Canada is to country as North America is to **continent**.
Word of the Day: We were careful not to break the **fragile** eggshell.
Think Tank: The frame measures 24 inches all the way around.
Brainteaser: Answers will vary.

Jumpstart 46

Magic Number: The magic number is in the hundreds place;
50,000 + 2,000 + 900 + 9; fifty-two thousand nine hundred nine
Math Busters:

Sentence Busters: 1. Today is November 3, 2002.
2. Have you ever seen a Canada goose?
Analogy of the Day: Salad is to fork as soup is to **spoon**.
Word of the Day: I spilled the **liquid** on my desk and got my papers wet.
Think Tank: Eileen had 1 cup left in the pitcher.
Brainteaser: Answers will vary.

Jumpstart 47

Magic Number: The magic number is in the hundreds place;
90,000 + 8,000 + 600 + 60 + 5; ninety-eight thousand six hundred sixty-five
Math Busters: 13 x 2 = 26; 22 x 4 = 88; 11 x 3 = 33
Sentence Busters: 1. What is the weather like in Florida?
2. I went to lots of museums in New York City.
Analogy of the Day: Bakery is to bread as butcher shop is to **meat**.
Word of the Day: I used a sponge to **absorb** all of the spilled milk.
Think Tank: $1.28 is shown. (Answers vary for second part of question.)
Brainteaser: Answers will vary.

Jumpstart 48

Magic Number: The magic number is in the ten-thousands place;
90,000 + 7,000 + 400 + 20 + 6; ninety-seven thousand four hundred twenty-six
Math Busters: The movie will start in one hour; The cookies will be done at 3:15 P.M.
Sentence Busters: 1. We wanted to buy plates, balloons, and streamers for our party. (Note: The comma after *balloons* is optional.) **2.** My watch tells time and it has an alarm.
Analogy of the Day: Cream cheese is to bagel as frosting is to **cake**.
Word of the Day: The teacher gave a **summary** of the book so the students would know what it was about.
Think Tank: Katherine has 32 shells in all.
Brainteaser: It took the second boat 12 more minutes to travel.

Jumpstart 49

Magic Number: The magic number is in the thousands place;
9,000 + 2; nine thousand two
Math Busters: 1 year = 12 months; 1 year = 365 days;
$\frac{1}{2}$ year = 6 months
Sentence Busters: 1. Three men went to the store.
2. The view from the mountain is beautiful.
Analogy of the Day: Shovel is to dig as knife is to **cut**.
Word of the Day: It is my **fantasy** to grow wings and fly around the world.
Think Tank: April, December, February, July, March, September
Brainteaser: Answers will vary.

Jumpstart 50

Magic Number: The magic number is in the ones place;
6,000 + 200 + 90 + 7; six thousand two hundred ninety-seven
Math Busters:

Sentence Busters: 1. October is the tenth month of the year.
2. My family gets together for Thanksgiving in November.
Analogy of the Day: Elephant is to big as mouse is to **small**.
Word of the Day: I love the way the stars **sparkle** at night like gems.
Think Tank: Seventy-two of the seeds did not grow.
Brainteaser: Answers will vary.